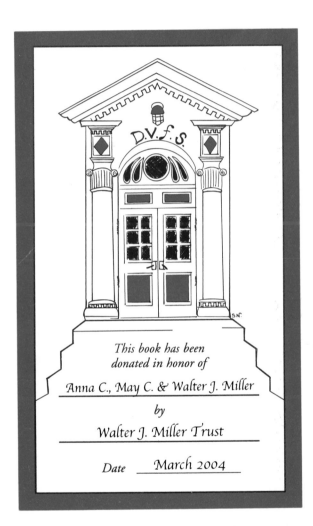

This book has been
donated in honor of

Anna C., May C. & Walter J. Miller

by

Walter J. Miller Trust

Date   March 2004

THE ANCIENT
AFRICAN
KINGDOM
OF
KUSH

*G*rateful acknowledgment is made to Joyce Haynes, Consultant in the Department of Ancient Egyptian, Nubian, and Near Eastern Art, Boston Museum of Fine Arts

THE ANCIENT
AFRICAN
KINGDOM
OF
KUSH

PAMELA F. SERVICE

BENCHMARK BOOKS

MARSHALL CAVENDISH
NEW YORK

FOR PETER AND ALL THE '69–'70 GANG AT MEROE.

Benchmark Books
Marshall Cavendish Corporation
99 White Plains Road
Tarrytown, New York 10591-9001

LIBRARY OF CONGRESS CATALOGING-IN-PUBLICATION DATA
Service, Pamela F.
The ancient African kingdom of Kush / by Pamela F. Service.
p.   cm. — (Cultures of the past)
Includes bibliographical references and index.
Summary: Examines the history, culture, religion, daily life, and the legends of the people of the
northern African kingdom of Kush, located in the region known as Nubia, between Sudan and Egypt.
ISBN 0-7614-0272-1 (lib. binding)
1. Nubia—Civilization—Juvenile literature. 2. Sudan—Civilization—Juvenile literature.
[1. Nubia. 2. Sudan.] I. Title. II. Series.
DT159.6.N83S47   1998   939'.78—dc20   96-34608   CIP   AC

Printed in Hong Kong

Photo research by Debbie Needleman

Front cover: An Egyptian king of the Twenty-fifth, or Kushite, Dynasty. The two cobras on his forehead
are believed to symbolize the Kushite claim to both Kush and Egypt.
Back cover: An Egyptian tomb painting from around 1400 B.C.E. Nubians are shown bringing the
Egyptian king tribute of gold, ebony logs, incense, and animal skins.

PHOTO CREDITS
Front cover: purchased by A.M. Lythgoe, courtesy of Museum of Fine Arts, Boston (04.1842); top
border on front cover, title page, and back cover and pages 26-27: from *Karanog: The Romano-Nubian
Cemetery*, text by C.L. Woolley and D. Randell-MacIver, Philadelphia: University Museum of the
University of Pennsylvania, 1910 (pl.27); page 6: The Image Bank/Neil Folberg; page 7: Martin Davies
Collection/Bridgeman Art Library, London; pages 9, 12, 29, 32, 48, 55 *(top left* and *top right)*, 56, 71:
Museum Expedition, courtesy of Museum of Fine Arts, Boston, (19.1572), (20.1059), (20.333),
(23.873), (23.731), (21.318), (15-3-421), (no accession #), (20.227); pages 10, 14, 16, 44-45, back
cover: copyright British Museum; page 13: Egyptian Expedition of The Metropolitan Museum of Art,
Rogers Fund, 1930 (30.4.21); page 19: Worcester Art Museum, Worcester, MA (1922.145); page 20:
Panos Pictures/Crispin Hughes; pages 21, 22, 38, 51, 52, 59: Aurora/Robert Caputo; page 24:
Aurora/Jose Azel; page 25: Director's Contingent Fund, courtesy of Museum of Fine Arts, Boston
(40.469); page 28: National Museum, Khartoum/Werner Forman/Art Resource, NY; pages 30, 37, 40,
53, 62, 63: Timothy Kendall; page 33: Meroitic alphabet from *Nubia, Ancient Kingdoms of Africa* by
Joyce Haynes, Boston: Museum of Fine Arts, 1992; pages 35, 39: Robert Frerck/Odyssey
Productions/Chicago; page 43: Bridgeman Art Library, London; pages 46, 47: from *Egypt and Nubia*,
vol. 1 (litho) by David Roberts (1796-1864), Stapleton Collection/Bridgeman Art Library, London;
page 55 *(bottom)*: Sudan Archaeological Museum, Khartoum/Werner Forman/Art Resource, NY; page
60: School of Archaeology, Classics & Oriental Studies, University of Liverpool (E8524); page 64:
Robert G. Service; page 67 *(left* and *right)*: Metropolitan Opera House, NY/Winnie Klotz; page 68:
Werner Forman/Art Resource, NY;
page 69: Susanne Gänsicke.

CONTENTS

CHAPTER ONE

ON THE RIVER OF HISTORY

Africa is the continent where, several million years ago, the human species began. It also became the home of some of humanity's earliest and most interesting civilizations. The North African kingdom of Kush was among the first of these.

A glance at a modern map will show no country called Kush today, but from around 2000 B.C.E. to 350 C.E.*, it existed along the river Nile in the northern part of what is now the nation of Sudan. To the north of this area was and is Egypt. Spanning the modern Egyptian/Sudanese border is a region today called Nubia, which at times was independent and at others was under Egyptian or Kushite control. The history of these regions along the Nile is closely intertwined in a long and important chapter of the human story.

The cataract around Aswan was the first of a series of rocky stretches along the Nile that made travel between Kush and Egypt difficult.

In the Beginning

Today, we think of North Africa as mostly desert, but ten thousand years ago it was a grassy plain. Wildlife was abundant and many people lived there by hunting and by gathering wild plants. The climate, however, began to grow drier until most of the animals and the people

*Many systems of dating have been used by different cultures throughout history. This series of books uses B.C.E. (Before Common Era) and C.E. (Common Era) instead of B.C. (Before Christ) and A.D. (Anno Domini) out of respect for the diversity of the world's peoples.

A nineteenth century painting by Edward Lear of the ruins at Philae. The island of Philae on the Nile was a place where Kush and Egypt met, both in their geography and in their religion. The goddess Isis, whose main temple was here, was revered in both countries.

who hunted them were forced to leave. Some moved eastward into the valley of the Nile.

The Nile, the world's longest river, carries life-giving water from the mountains and forests of East Africa northward to the Mediterranean Sea. The African people who settled in the Nile Valley found that, besides hunting, they could raise livestock and grow crops in the rich soil. Instead of living as nomads, wandering from place to place chasing game for food, they could settle down, develop their government and religion, and create things that were beautiful as well as useful.

At its northern end, where the river nears the Mediterranean Sea, the Nile Valley was broader and many crops could be grown there. The people became prosperous and some began living in cities. They built ships and were in contact with other peoples around the Mediterranean, exchanging goods and ideas.

Farther south, beyond modern Aswan, the Nile crossed through a series of cataracts, rocky stretches where the river was churned into foam, and travel by land or water was difficult. This region, now called Nubia, had less land that could be farmed, and the people living there were less prosperous and had little contact with the cultures to their north.

Today nobody knows what these people called themselves. Archaeologists in Nubia use letters of the alphabet when talking about ancient peoples. This early group is referred to, rather unimaginatively, as the A Group.

Neighbors on the Nile

Around 3100 B.C.E., the peoples of the north united to form the kingdom of Egypt. South of there, in the cataract area, the peoples of Nubia struggled to remain independent and continue developing their own cultures. For eight hundred years (during Egypt's Early Dynastic and Old Kingdom periods), the Egyptians and the Nubians were often at war.

When the Egyptians were victorious, they recorded the number of cattle and prisoners captured. During more peaceful times, they recorded the trade goods brought from Nubia or through Nubia from farther south in Africa. These included ivory, rare woods, wild animals, animal skins, precious minerals, and the eggs and feathers of ostriches. Gold and gems from the desert hills were particularly treasured. The Egyptians also went into Nubia to quarry special stones for making statues and, at times, Nubian soldiers, who were particularly valued as archers, were taken into the Egyptian army.

Then came a period when Egypt's central government fell apart, and Egyptians were too busy squabbling among themselves to pay attention to Nubia. At this same time, around 2000 B.C.E., a new group of Nubians became dominant there. Archaeologists call them the C Group. It might be easier to remember this by imagining that the C stands for cattle, since cattle were particularly important to these people.

Cattle were very important to the C Group people of Nubia (2000–1550 B.C.E.), who often buried clay figures of cattle with their dead.

When Egypt again grew strong (during the Middle Kingdom period) and decided to expand southward, its armies met fierce resistance from the C Group and related peoples. The Egyptians were forced to build a number of military forts between the first and second cataracts.

Kush Appears on the Scene

During this time, Egyptian records first mentioned Kush as a community south of the third cataract, with its capital at Kerma. Its strength and considerable wealth came partly from controlling the gold mines as well as the river and land routes for African goods going to Egypt.

Around 1795 B.C.E., a Middle Eastern people called the Hyksos conquered much of Egypt. The Egyptian forts in Nubia were abandoned, and the ruler of Kerma took advantage of this to extend his territory northward. The Hyksos king wasn't interested in conquering Nubia, but when he

PEOPLE OF THE BOW

The people of Kush and Nubia were known for their skill as archers. The earliest Egyptian hieroglyphic sign for Nubia was a picture of a bow, and Nubian archers were often hired by the Egyptian army. Kushite kings, queens, and gods were often shown clutching bows and arrows.

Not only were bows and arrows important to the living, they frequently were buried with the dead. Quivers were mostly made of leather; arrow shafts were of wood or cane; and the arrowheads were often metal, although some continued to be chipped from stone. In one Kushite grave a bronze quiver was found that contained seventy-three arrows whose tips had apparently been dipped in poison.

The Kushites, like some Nile tribes today, pulled the bowstring back with their thumbs instead of their forefingers. In order to draw the taut bowstrings extra far without cutting themselves, the Kushites wore wide stone rings on their thumbs. Many thumb rings have been found in graves, and wall carvings show Kushite kings, queens, and gods wearing them. Some tribes along the Nile and to its west still wear thumb rings during ceremonies.

In 430 B.C.E., the Greek historian Herodotus wrote about spies sent a century earlier to Kush by Persia's King Cambyses. The Kushite king gave them a powerful local bow and said, "When the Persians can pull a bow of this strength easily, then let them come with an army of superior strength." The Persians never came back.

This painted jug from Kush shows one of the country's famed archers in action.

heard of a prince in southern Egypt rebelling against him, he wrote the ruler of Kerma (whose name may have been Nedjeh) suggesting that the Hyksos and Kerma join forces against this rebellious prince and divide Egypt between them.

The Egyptian prince intercepted the letter, however, and eventually he and his sons threw the Hyksos out, reuniting all of Egypt. Thus began the prosperous period of Egyptian history known as the New Kingdom.

Egypt's now powerful armies pushed their frontier southward to the fourth cataract and destroyed the city of Kerma. Egyptians built settlements and temples throughout Nubia, and the Nubians were forced to send regular tribute to Egypt. The Egyptian viceroy there was called "The King's Son of Kush." Nubian soldiers again served in Egypt's armies, and the sons of Nubian leaders were taken north to be educated so that they would accept Egyptian ways. It was during this New Kingdom period, from 1550–1085 B.C.E., that Egypt's influence in Nubia was greatest.

Kush Conquers Egypt

With the end of the New Kingdom, Egypt fell into another time of weakness and withdrew from Nubia. Meanwhile, Kush was reestablishing itself, placing its capital at Napata, a city upriver from Kerma, near the fourth cataract. By then, the Kushites had adopted many Egyptian ways. With Egypt now weak and under the influence of various foreign powers, the kings of Kush decided that they were the rightful preservers of the Egyptian state and its traditions.

Shortly before 750 B.C.E., King Kashta of Kush led his armies into Egypt. He conquered the southern Egyptian city of Thebes and made his daughter, Amenirdis, priestess of Amon, Egypt's chief god. His sons, Piankhy and then Shabako, continued into northern Egypt, threw out its Libyan rulers, and declared themselves kings of Egypt. This period of Kushite kings became known as Egypt's Twenty-fifth Dynasty.

During this time, Kush ruled a vast area stretching from the Mediterranean to well south of modern Khartoum. For Egypt, it was a period of peace and prosperity. Taharqa, who ruled from 699–663 B.C.E., was a strong king, but all during his reign, he faced trouble abroad. He worked with neighboring states through diplomacy and military alliances, trying to counter the growing power of Assyria, a kingdom near the eastern end of

A golden mask of Queen Malakaye who, in the early sixth century B.C.E., was married to a Napatan king.

the Mediterranean. These efforts failed, and the Assyrians conquered one state after another, finally turning to Egypt.

The Assyrians Move In

In 671 B.C.E., Assyria attacked Egypt. On and off over seventeen years, battles raged back and forth. Eventually, Taharqa was driven back into Kush, but his nephew and successor, Tanwetamani, marched north again and retook Egypt. The Assyrians returned under King Ashurbanipal, attacked a number of Egyptian cities, and, finally, brought an end to the Twenty-fifth Dynasty and the Kushite rule of Egypt.

The Assyrian destruction of Thebes was recalled fifty years later in the Bible when the prophet Nahum forecast a similar fate for others: "Art thou better than No-Amon [Thebes], that was situated among the arms of the Nile and that had the waters around her: whose rampart and wall was the river? Kush and Egypt were her strength . . . Yet she, too, went into

In this Egyptian tomb painting from around 1360 B.C.E., Nubians carry rich tribute to Egypt's king. The yellow rings on the trays represent gold.

A stone sphinx of Taharqa showing the Kushite king with a lion body and a human head. The sphinx was an Egyptian image that the Twenty-fifth Dynasty kings adopted, but they used a double cobra rather than a single one on the forehead, perhaps to show that they ruled two kingdoms, Kush and Egypt.

captivity; her young children were dashed in pieces at the corners of all the streets. Lots were cast for her honorable men, and all her great men were bound in chains."

Egypt was next ruled by Egyptian allies of the Assyrians, and then by a series of weak or foreign-dominated dynasties. The kings and queens of Kush, however, still considered themselves the rightful rulers of Egypt. They continued to use the titles and regalia of Egyptian royalty for the next nine hundred years.

Rule from Meroe

Relations between Kush and the rulers of Egypt were sometimes good but more often bad. In 591 B.C.E., the Egyptians attacked and sacked Napata, the Kushite capital. At this point, Aspelta, king of Kush, decided to move out of harm's way and established his country's political capital farther south, in the prosperous town of Meroe (MARE-o-way).

Sixty-six years later, Cambyses, the Persian king who then ruled Egypt, sent spies to Meroe. They were impressed enough by what they saw, and by Kush's soldiers during a border skirmish, to decide not to invade Kush. Kushite troops were even hired to serve in Persia's army.

Meroe's governors managed affairs in Nubia, and often the children of Nubian leaders were sent south to live for a while at Meroe to strengthen ties between the northern and southern parts of the kingdom. For two more centuries, though, Napata remained the religious capital, and the kings and queens returned there to be crowned and to be buried.

A Greek historian recorded the event that probably ended that tradition. The priests of the god Amon had been very powerful in Napata; they even had the power to make the king commit suicide if they disagreed with him. However, when they tried that with King Arakakamani around 280 B.C.E., he showed up at the Amon temple with his army and had the priests killed instead. From then on, the rulers of Kush were crowned and buried at Meroe.

The Greek king Alexander the Great conquered Egypt in 332 B.C.E., and one of his generals, Ptolemy, founded a line of Greek-Egyptian rulers. Sometimes troubles flared between the rulers of Kush and the Ptolemies, but at other times they got along well enough to work together on building projects in Nubia.

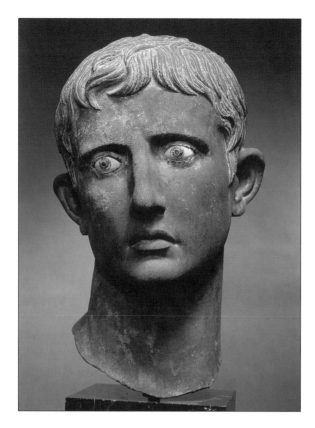

This bronze head from a statue of Rome's Emperor Augustus was probably a trophy brought back to Meroe by Queen Amanirenas and Prince Akinidad after their raid on a Roman fort in 24 B.C.E.

In 30 B.C.E., the independence of ancient Egypt came to an end with the death of Cleopatra VII, and Egypt became a part of the Roman Empire. Local leaders in Roman-controlled Nubia objected to Roman taxes and launched a minor rebellion. Thinking this was their chance to again extend their territory northward, the Kushite queen Amanirenas and her son, Akinidad, marched north. In 24 B.C.E., they attacked Roman-Egyptian forts near the first cataract. They toppled statues of Rome's Emperor Augustus Caesar and carried the head of one statue back to Meroe, burying it ceremonially under the doorway of a temple.

Rome, however, was then the strongest military power in the world and, the next year, the Roman general Petronius led an army against the Kushites, driving them back south and burning Napata, their former capital. The Romans stopped there, however, and the terms of the peace treaty were surprisingly favorable to Kush. This suggests that Rome had developed a respect for the strength of Kush and decided not to extend its empire farther south than Egypt.

A NAME FROM AFRICA'S PAST

Do you know someone named Candace? If so, you have an ancient link to the kingdom of Kush.

In the Kushite language, Candace (probably pronounced KAN-DA-key) was a title for Queen or Queen Mother. Outsiders referring to a Kushite queen often confused her title with her name and called her Queen Candace. When, year after year, the ruler was Candace, they sometimes assumed this was one very long-lived woman.

When the Romans fought the armies of Candace and her son in 23 B.C.E., this was probably Queen Amanirenas. In the next century, Amanikhatashan was probably the queen who met the spies sent by Rome's Emperor Nero.

She may also have been the Candace referred to in the Bible (Acts VIII, 26–37). This Candace sent a delegation to Jerusalem where one member was baptized by the Apostle Paul. It was from this biblical account that the ancient African title for queen became one of the names we use today.

Kush enjoyed a period of great prosperity during the centuries around the turn of the era. The Kushites used no coinage, but trade flourished as they exchanged their own products and those from farther south for goods from Egypt, Rome, Arabia, and even India. The kings and queens built temples throughout the kingdom, and local crafts such as metalworking and pottery flourished.

The Fall of Kush

But enemies who had troubled Kush throughout its history were gaining strength. For more than a thousand years, Kushite monuments had often shown rulers defeating hostile tribesmen from the east and the west. At Jebel Qeili such a pictorial record is carved on a rock outcrop way out in the eastern desert. Over the centuries, North Africa had been growing drier, and desert tribes kept trying to force their way into the rich Nile Valley. At the same time, the decline

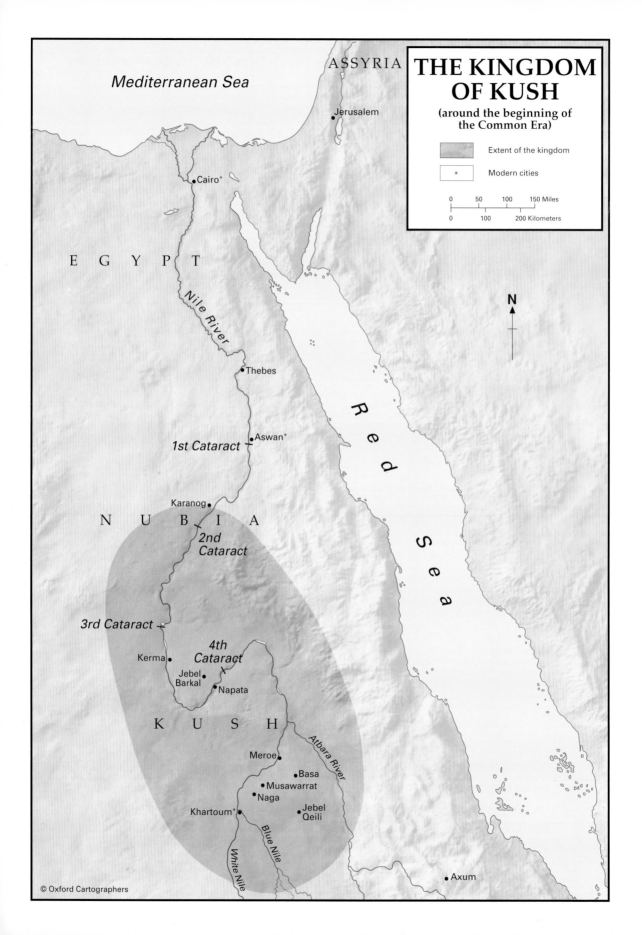

THE KINGDOM OF KUSH
(around the beginning of the Common Era)

Extent of the kingdom

* Modern cities

0   50   100   150 Miles
0   100   200 Kilometers

Mediterranean Sea

ASSYRIA

Jerusalem

Cairo*

EGYPT

Nile River

Thebes

Aswan*

1st Cataract

Karanog

NUBIA

2nd Cataract

3rd Cataract

Kerma

4th Cataract

Jebel Barkal

Napata

KUSH

Meroe

Basa

Musawarrat

Naga

Khartoum*

Jebel Qeili

Atbara River

White Nile

Blue Nile

Red Sea

Axum

N

© Oxford Cartographers

of the Roman Empire reduced the trade coming into Kush.

Then around 350 C.E., Ezana, king of Axum, a powerful new kingdom east of Kush, made his second attack on Kush. By then much of Kush was being controlled by people called the Noba. Meroe and other cities were burned. Many aspects of Kushite culture survived into the Christian and Islamic periods that followed. But the kingdom of Kush, after several thousand years, had come to an end.

Kushite Prince Arikankharer bashes his enemies. The lion in the lower right corner of the stone plaque is probably symbolic of the Kushite warrior god Apedemek.

CHAPTER TWO

AN AFRICAN WAY OF LIFE

At first glance, the culture of Kush looks far more Egyptian than African. The royal pyramids and temples to animal-headed gods certainly seem to be based on Egyptian models.

Yet both Egypt and Kush grew from the same African foundation. The Kushites didn't seem to feel they were adopting anything particularly foreign when they took on Egyptian ways, remodeling them to fit their own African life.

The importance of cattle to the modern Dinka people is seen by this man singing praise songs to one of his favorite animals. The Dinka today live on the Nile south of ancient Kush but seem to share the Kushites' fondness for cattle.

Making a Living

One early difference between Kush and Egypt was the basis of their economies. Both countries were on the Nile, a river that floods every summer when it carries a big surge of rainwater from East Africa. Mud flowed along with the water and, when the floods went down, that mud was left on the farm fields, making them good for growing crops.

In Egypt, particularly in the north, the floodplains were wide, and strong central governments produced even more good farmland by draining swamps and building irrigation canals.

In Nubia, however, the river valley was narrow and rocky. Farming did not create as much wealth as in Egypt. Grazing livestock in the valley and on the fringes of the desert was very important.

The Nubian C Group peoples were largely herdsmen. They drew pictures of cattle on rocks in areas that were probably grassier than

Cattle were very important in the lives of ancient Kushites just as they still are to the Nuer people who live on the Nile south of ancient Kush. This type of cattle is very like the type shown in carvings and paintings of ancient Kush and Egypt.

today. They also buried their dead with cattle skulls and clay models of cattle, and they placed stone pillars with cattle carved on them near graves.

During this same time (2000–1550 B.C.E.), the Nubian people of the Kerma culture shared this same tradition. Individuals showed their wealth not only in gold and beautiful objects but also in the number of cattle they owned. As many as four hundred cattle might be slaughtered at the death of a ruler and buried near his grave mound. Offerings and ceremonies involving milk were part of the religion.

Cattle continued to be important during the Napatan period (800–591 B.C.E.), but there wasn't enough good grazing land around Napata to support the number of cattle that a wealthy kingdom such as Kush wanted to have.

This may be another reason why the capital was moved south to Meroe.

Meroe is also on the Nile, but in an area far enough south so as not to depend totally on the river for water. Unlike Egypt and Nubia, it enjoys a summer rainy season when the usually dry hills and plains are green with grass, and water flows down what normally are dry valleys, or *wadis*.

On the flatlands along the river, villagers in the region of Meroe raised crops of millet, vegetables, dates, and cotton. Because of the natural rainfall, these farmers made little use of the ox-driven waterwheel that was introduced in Meroitic times. However, Nubia had been suffering from periods when the Nile was low, and this device that lifted water from the Nile

This modern Sudanese village near the ruins of ancient Meroe has rectangular, flat-roofed houses of mud brick, very like those lived in by the Kushites thousands of years ago.

into irrigation ditches made possible flourishing settlements in Meroitic Nubia.

The people of Kush, particularly in the south, included a number of nomadic herdsmen. In the *wadis*, rainwater reservoirs were built for watering the herds of sheep, goats, and cattle. These also served as stopping places for caravans following trade routes between Kush and areas to its east.

Kushites kept cattle partly as a visual measure of their wealth, but beef was also important in their diet, as the great many cattle bones found at Meroitic sites show. Milk and dairy products were valued as well in the daily diet and in religious ceremonies. Milk was collected in tightly woven reed baskets of a type still used farther south on the Nile and, like those same modern tribes, Kushites drank their milk out of bowls. Bronze bells were worn by one or more cows in a herd. Beautiful examples of these bells have been found in graves in which the dead person was buried with several favorite animals.

According to Herodotus, the Greek historian, when the king of Kush, in 525 B.C.E., was trying to impress Persian spies with the strength of his people, he told them that Kushites lived one hundred and twenty years due to their diet of boiled meat and milk.

An interesting African tradition seen in Kush was the occasional deforming of cattle horns. One or both of a young animal's horns would be deliberately shaped to grow in an unnatural way. This was done at least from C Group to Meroitic times and is still practiced by some peoples living farther south on the Nile. Herdsmen today say they do it to make an animal more beautiful and to mark it as a special favorite.

Kushite Homes

In riverside towns and villages, most of the people of Kush lived in rectangular brick homes. Wealthier people built with hard fire-brick while others used bricks made from sunbaked mud. Most homes had several rooms, and one style included a courtyard on the east where work could be done in the morning sunlight before the day got too hot. Roofs were flat and supported by beams of palm or acacia trees.

In the capital city of Meroe, royalty and members of the court lived in large buildings of stone or fire-brick. This area of town was surrounded by a stone wall and may have originally been built on a small island before river

FUN IN KUSH

Archaeology can do more than tell us about kings and pottery. It can help answer questions such as "What did the people of Kush do for fun?"

Men, and probably some women, went horseback riding, drove chariots, hunted, fished, and practiced archery. These activities were often part of their everyday work, but they probably enjoyed them too, and sometimes may have done them just for fun.

The harp and flute—musical instruments known in Egypt, Greece, and Rome—were also played in Kush. We know that there was dancing in some ceremonies because pictures on pottery and a chapel wall show people doing a dance that is still popular in parts of Sudan. In this dance, someone beats a drum hung around the neck while others dance about waving palm fronds, thrusting their heads back and puffing out their chests.

Kushites probably did many other things for fun that left little trace, such as storytelling and singing. But we do know that they liked playing games.

Tombs of Kerma, Napata, and Meroe have produced dice and carved gaming pieces. Common finds on most sites are round disks ground down from broken pieces of pottery and probably used in a game similar to checkers. On a stone in the wall that surrounds Meroe's royal city, and on another stone near the cemeteries, rows of holes have been pecked out for what looks like the game of *wari*, still popular in much of Africa. In this game, the aim is to move the most pebbles through a series of holes. We can imagine bored guards sneaking a game when their commander wasn't looking.

Besides games, Kushite children also played with toys. Many were probably made of wood or straw and haven't lasted, but excavations where the ordinary Meroites lived have uncovered pottery horses, cattle, and people, some of which were probably toys. There were clay balls and small round stones that may have been used like marbles. Archaeologists have also found a number of marble-sized clay heads with holes in their bottoms. They may have been meant to be stuck on sticks for use as dolls.

All this shows that wherever and whenever people live, they always find ways to have fun.

Wari has been a popular game in Africa for thousands of years. Scenes like this modern one would have been common in ancient Kush as well.

This leather-strung wooden bed from a tomb at Kerma is decorated with ivory inlays, but otherwise it is similar to beds still made in Sudan.

channels shifted. It boasted tree-lined avenues and, later, a public bathhouse of the Roman type, decorated with Roman-style statues.

Craftsmen, merchants, and ordinary citizens lived in neighborhoods to the north and south of the royal enclosure, while the industrial area where iron smelting and pottery making took place was to the east. Because the most common houses were made of easily crumbled mud-brick, new homes were continually being built on the remains of older ones. Mounds of remains and household rubbish rose in places to thirty-three feet (ten meters) in height and spanned a period of well over a thousand years.

Wood seldom survives in archaeological sites, but we do know what some furniture was like because examples were placed in graves. Rope-strung beds and wooden headrests were used in Kush just as they were in ancient Egypt and in many parts of Africa today. The usual furnishings found in house-remains include clay ovens, tall water pots, and large, flat, bread-making pans. Similar items can still be found in nearby Sudanese homes, except that today the bread pans are made of aluminum instead of clay.

All of the people of ancient Kush were not farmers or city dwellers who stayed in one place. Many were herdsmen who traveled with their animals in search of grass and water. These nomadic people lived in beehive-shaped huts that could be taken down and moved quickly. They were covered by reeds or animal skins, and some had ostrich eggs placed, perhaps as lucky charms, on their roofs. Similar huts and even ostrich egg charms can still be found farther south on the Nile.

Such houses usually leave little evidence in archaeological sites, but depictions of them have been found on a temple wall at Meroe, at the Amon temple at Jebel Barkal, near Napata, and on a beautiful bronze bowl from Karanog in Meroitic Nubia. Some of the sites in the *wadis* east of Meroe, which now show only ruins of temples and reservoirs, may once have been surrounded by such huts.

Pottery

One of the things most frequently found in the city mounds of Meroe and at most archaeological sites is pottery. Archaeologists talk a lot about pottery, not because it was the most important thing in the lives of ancient people but because it lasts longer than many other things people use. Also, different groups of people tend to make different styles of pottery so, by studying the pottery found in a place, it is often possible to figure out which people lived there and with whom they traded.

The early African settlers in the Nile Valley made pottery by coiling up

This scene on a bronze bowl found at Karnog in Meroitic Nubia gives an interesting picture of Kushite life. A plump, important woman sits in front of her round reed hut with an ostrich egg charm on its roof. Her drinking bowls are being filled by a herdsman who has brought his cattle, some with artistically deformed horns. A boy uses a basket to milk a cow who affectionately licks his ear.

rolls of clay, rubbing the surface smooth, then decorating the vessel with scratches and jabs. Today very similar pottery is still handmade for every-day use in Sudan and other parts of Africa. The people who make it are usually women.

When the use of the potter's wheel was introduced, finer pottery making became a profession that demanded more time than could be given by women busy with their many household tasks. Men became professional potters. Their wares were not meant for daily household use but were sold and sometimes were traded over long distances. The styles of this wheel-made pottery changed as new fashions or foreign styles became popular.

Throughout the history of Kush, many types of pottery were used. The handmade type continued largely unchanged while different wheel-made styles were developed locally or introduced from outside. During the Meroitic period, Kush produced what is considered some of the finest pottery ever made in the ancient world.

This pottery, wheel-made from fine white clay, is hard, thin, and beau-tifully decorated. It is either stamped with repeated decorations or painted in lively free-flowing designs. Some patterns were inspired by Egyptian or Roman ideas, while others are original designs or delightful drawings of animals and people.

The Role of Women

Another very African feature of Kushite culture was the important role women played. In Egypt, as in many Mediterranean countries, women were generally kept subordinate to men in government and society, and they

The Meroitic king and queen shown here making offerings to Amon and Isis are unidentified. If the Meroitic inscription underneath could be read, it would be possible to understand what this stone slab is recording.

seldom ruled as queens in their own right. But in Kush, as in many African societies, women enjoyed more power and equality.

Unlike Egypt, inheritance was passed through the women, as is still done today in many African societies. The heir to the throne of Kush was not always the king's son but often the son of his mother or his sister. The king's mother was considered especially important. When Taharqa was crowned in Egypt, he sent to Napata for his mother, so that she could see him crowned. Later kings recorded similar efforts. And in Kush, particularly in Meroitic times, it was fairly common for queens to rule in their own right or on equal footing with their sons or husbands.

It is probable that women had more power among ordinary people, too. In the bowl from Karanog (depicted on pages 26–27), a woman sits outside a hut, receiving offerings of cattle and milk as if she were a local person of importance.

The African Look

We can form an idea of what the people of Kush looked like by studying the skeletons found in graves and by looking at Egyptian and Kushite statues and reliefs.

They were apparently similar to some of the people living in northern Sudan today. Generally, they were dark-skinned with tightly curled hair, broad noses, and full lips. They also had a more African than Mediterranean attitude toward physical beauty.

In ancient Egypt, a slender body was thought the height of beauty, and all men and women were shown that way whether they looked like that in real life or not. In Kush, however, particularly in Meroitic times, big was considered beautiful.

Kushite queens, princesses, and goddesses were shown as being very ample, and the men and gods were also depicted as much stockier than in Egypt. Special emphasis is even made of the fat creases around their necks. The woman being offered milk in the Karanog bowl is quite plump. This suggests similarities to recent practices in the southern Nile area where

Kushite metalworkers were skilled craftsmen, using Egyptian themes with their own bold sense of design. This intricately hinged bracelet of gold and enamel, showing the goddess Hathor, comes from Jebel Barkal in the first century B.C.E.

This young woman from a village near the ancient site of Jebel Barkal wears facial scars similar to those shown in Kush. Several patterns were used in both past and present, and the reasons for using them may have been similar: group identification, medical treatment, and beauty.

men show their importance by deliberately fattening their wives with lots of milk.

This way of portraying the rulers not only expressed their beauty in Kushite eyes, but also indicated that they were so rich and powerful they could afford to eat whatever they wanted and didn't have to do manual labor. This is probably also why Kushite women are shown with long fingernails, a luxury of women who had servants to do their household work.

The clothes Kushite rulers and gods were shown wearing, particularly during the Meroitic period, are also different from the simpler Egyptian styles. Both men and women wore long patterned robes with tasseled cords and pleated sashes that draped from one shoulder. And they wore lots of jewelry, including large earrings, rings on nearly every finger, beaded collars, heavy necklaces, and many bracelets and armbands. One type of amulet they are shown wearing is very similar to a good luck charm worn by many Sudanese children today. Crowns, though basically Egyptian in style, had their own Kushite details. The swords of kings and queens, instead of being worn at the belt, were slung across the chest in a way still seen among some North African peoples.

Another very African feature of the Kushites was that many of them had deliberate facial scars. Most often these were three vertical scars on the cheeks. Such Kushite faces are shown on pots, on clay coffins, and even on little clay doll heads. On wall reliefs, several kings and queens are shown wearing them. The use of facial scars for decoration, tribal identification, and medical treatment (particularly for eye problems) is still common in modern Africa. Some Sudanese living near the ruins of Meroe still wear the three-scar pattern of ancient Kush.

Altogether, the picture we have of the Kushites is of a self-confident African people who enjoyed elaborate display and who took pride in themselves.

Language

We would know a lot more about the people of Kush, about their history and beliefs, if we were able to understand their language. Unfortunately, Meroitic is one of the few ancient languages that today can be pronounced but not understood.

During Napatan times, the official language of government and religion was Egyptian. Documents and monument inscriptions were written in Egyptian hieroglyphics. Probably people spoke their own native language for everyday use and, in time, even the priests and scribes forgot the fine points of Egyptian spelling and grammar.

When the capital was moved from Napata to Meroe, many things became more distinctly Kushite, including the writing. New hieroglyphic and cursive writing systems were developed and were used for writing Meroitic, the language spoken at least by Kush's ruling class.

The writing systems were simpler than the Egyptian ones. They were purely alphabetic, went in one direction only, and had dots separating words.

Today it is possible to figure out the Meroitic alphabet because inscriptions were found in which names of people were written in both Egyptian and Meroitic. Since the Egyptian could be read, it was possible to learn the sound values for the written Meroitic signs. But today, spoken Meroitic has totally died out. Although we can pronounce the language, we do not know what the words mean.

Scholars hope that someday the puzzle of the Meroitic language will be solved. This could happen if inscriptions are found written in both Meroitic and some other language that we know, such as Egyptian, Greek, or Latin. Or perhaps in studying modern African languages, we may find one related to ancient Meroitic that can give us clues to the meanings of words. In any case, reading the lost language of Kush would help fill in many pieces in our picture of that great kingdom.

Offering tables in Kush and Egypt were placed on the east sides of graves for priests and mourners to make offerings to the dead. This one for Meroitic Prince Tedegen has the usual scene of the god and goddess of funerals presenting fruit, cakes, and milk, but the usual prayer is in Meroitic, not Egyptian. Comparing these prayers in both languages made it possible to learn the letters and a few words in Meroitic.

WRITING MEROITIC

Although the Meroitic language cannot yet be read, we do have a pretty good idea of its alphabet. At first, hieroglyphic writing was used for formal inscriptions, but cursive script was easier to write and soon took over.

Here is an approximation of the Meroitic hieroglyphic and cursive alphabets. We may not be able to read this language yet, but we can have fun using its letters to write our own.

Hieroglyph	Cursive	Phonetic value	Hieroglyph	Cursive	Phonetic value
		a			l
		e			kh
		i			kh
		o			sh
		y			s (se)
		w			k
		b			q
		p			t
		m			te
		n			to
		ne			d
		r			word divider

CHAPTER THREE

THE AFRO-EGYPTIAN WORLD

Many of the religious beliefs and practices of Kush were similar to those of ancient Egypt. But it is hard to tell how much of this was because of Egyptian influence in Kush and how much was because both cultures rose from the same base. Since Kushite culture was distinct in many ways, it would be wrong to assume that some religious similarities meant that everything was the same. So to build a picture of Kushite religion, we must turn not only to what we know of Egyptian beliefs, but also to archaeology.

Divine Order

It is often said that our modern world worships change. We love anything new and are always looking for new fashions and for new and faster ways to do things. To us, change is natural and good.

The ancient peoples of the Nile Valley saw it very differently. Their ideal world was orderly and predictable. Change disturbed this ideal and was therefore considered bad.

The people of the Nile did not share the thinking of many Mediterranean peoples who felt that the world was divided into good and evil, with each side always trying to overcome the other. Instead, they felt that everything was of some value and had its place in the world. There was a balance and order to life, and things went wrong when these were broken. They even had a goddess of balance and order, of *rightness*. Her name was Ma'at.

This is similar to beliefs held by some African peoples today. And it is understandable because life along the Nile was very predictable. Once a year the river flooded, covering the fields with life-giving mud and allowing crops to be grown for another year. The weather was generally warm and sunny, and people's lives were seldom troubled by unexpected events such as rainstorms, tornadoes, or earthquakes.

This painting from a New Kingdom Egyptian tomb shows Osiris, king of the dead, with the false beard, crown, and crook and flail of an Egyptian king. Egyptian artists often colored dead people green.

Land of Many Gods

For the people of the Nile Valley, the sun and the river Nile were both seen as unchanging life-giving forces, and both were worshiped as gods who helped create the world. Other gods then came into being and established life as the ancient peoples came to know it.

In Egypt and in Kush, it was believed that the god Osiris was made king of this world by the creator gods. Later, he was killed by his jealous brother, Set, who chopped up Osiris's body and scattered the pieces. Osiris's loving wife, Isis, searched for the pieces, sewed them together, and brought Osiris back to life. He then went on to rule in the afterworld, and his son, Horus, took over ruling this one.

But they did not have to rule these worlds alone. The people of the ancient Nile believed in hundreds of gods. Every town had its own gods and local versions of more general gods. And when foreigners came in, the gods they brought with them were often adopted, too.

The gods and goddesses usually had some particular duties or were in charge of certain places. Examples of the hundreds of gods recognized in both Egypt and Kush include Thoth, an ibis-headed man who was the god of scribes, and Taweret, a hippopotamus standing upright who looks very like a pregnant woman and was, appropriately, the goddess of childbirth. The cat goddess, Bastet, had several duties, one of which was to be special guardian of the southern Egyptian town of Bubastis.

Sometimes, several gods seemed to have had the same duties, or one god might have had various unrelated duties. This may have come about because people living in different places created different gods to take care of the same thing, or several local gods with different jobs might be joined to form one god.

All this is confusing to us today, but it never seemed to bother the ancient people of the Nile. They were easygoing and accepting in their beliefs, and since absolute good and evil were not part of their thinking, they were willing to say that anyone might have some good ideas. As far as they were concerned, the more gods, the merrier.

Egyptian Gods in Kush

For thousands of years, Nubians traded with Egypt, served in or fought against Egyptian armies, or were under Egyptian colonial control. Since they already shared many of the basic beliefs, it is hardly surprising that these southerners adopted some gods of their more powerful neighbors, sometimes blending them with their own gods.

During the New Kingdom (1550–1085 B.C.E.), when Egypt directly controlled parts of Nubia, the most powerful god, the one most closely associated with strong kingship, was Amon. His sacred animal was the ram, also sacred to some Nubian gods, and the center of his worship was at the capital, Thebes, in southern Egypt. The Amon priesthood was politically very powerful, and temples to that god were built throughout Egypt and

The people of the Nile lived very close to the natural world, and even the humblest creatures could symbolize something important in their beliefs.

Frogs are an example. In Egyptian mythology, frogs were among the first creatures to rise from the original sea. In one creation myth, frogs and snakes living in the primordial mud cared for an egg from which hatched the sun god, making the rest of creation possible.

Perhaps because of this association with the beginning of life, a frog-headed goddess, named Heket, was the special protector of midwives, women who assist at childbirth. Heket's husband was one of the creator gods, and the center of their worship was near the Nubian-Egyptian border.

In Kush, the frog was particularly popular. It is sometimes painted on fine Meroitic pottery, often along with the *ankh* sign for life, but not all Kushite frogs were small. Large stone statues of frogs were put around some of the reservoirs in the *wadis* east of Meroe.

The ancient Egyptians believed that frogs hatched each year from newly fertilized Nile mud, and the Kushites apparently extended that idea to their desert reservoirs. They noticed that frog eggs would hatch with the next year's rains, so the frog was clearly the right creature to ask to protect reservoirs and to bring abundant rain.

The old reservoirs are now largely filled with wind-blown dirt. But at least one stone frog stands in greenery again. It was taken from the desert site of Basa to Khartoum, the capital of modern Sudan. There it graces gardens at the Sudan National Museum.

This stone frog once guarded a reservoir near Musawwarat.

Egyptian Nubia. One of the southernmost was at Jebel Barkal across the river from the town of Napata.

The earlier Kushite Kingdom at Kerma recognized some Egyptian gods, but mostly their religion was that of the local cattle-herding people. But after the collapse of Egypt's New Kingdom—when the capital of Kush was established at Napata—Amon, with his large temple at Jebel Barkal, also became the state god of Kush.

When these Napatan kings invaded Egypt and began the Twenty-fifth Dynasty, they were anxious to prove themselves "more Egyptian than the Egyptians" and stressed their devotion to the Egyptian gods, especially Amon. They put up inscriptions and built temples all over their now very large kingdom, even as far south as Meroe.

The political power of Amon and his priesthood was reduced when

This ram is part of a row of statues that leads up to the Temple of Amon at Jebel Barkal. The ram was sacred to Amon.

Isis, chief goddess of both Kush and Egypt, here leads Egypt's king Ramses III (ca. 1160 B.C.E.) through the trials he faces after death.

King Arakakamani killed the priests who ordered his suicide and moved his religious capital to Meroe. Nonetheless, the Amon Temple at Meroe, built just outside the royal enclosure, was continually enlarged throughout Meroitic times. It was there that the later kings and queens of Meroe were crowned.

A great many other Egyptian gods appeared in Kushite inscriptions and on reliefs, though few had their own temples. An exception was the goddess Isis. The rulers of Kush called her their "mother." She was frequently shown on temples around Meroe and had temples of her own in Nubia. Her popularity in Kush is hardly surprising since Isis was also adopted by the Romans in Egypt and became popular throughout the Roman Empire.

The lion god Apedemek was worshiped only by the Kushites. Both a warrior god and a creator god, he is shown here associated with a lotus and a snake, both part of the creation myths common to the early people of the Nile.

The Gods of Kush

As was true in the rest of the Nile Valley, Kush had many local gods and goddesses. When the royal capital was established at Meroe, some of the gods of that region rose to importance in the Kushite state. Chief among these was Apedemek, the lion god.

Lions were associated with several minor gods and goddesses in Egypt and Nubia, but only with the rise of Meroe did a lion god achieve great importance. Lions were still known in that area during the nineteenth century C.E., and in Kushite times they must have been a powerful and dangerous fact of life.

At Meroe and sites to its east, temples were built to Apedemek. He was primarily a warrior god and a special protector of the royal family and the Kushite state. He also seems to have some association with creation and with the sun. In some Meroitic temples, Apedemek was considered important enough to replace Osiris in groupings with Isis and Horus.

Usually Apedemek appears as a muscular lion-headed man clad in armor, clutching a bow or sword, and defeating enemies. In one unusual wall relief, he is shown with three heads and four arms presenting symbols of life and abundance to the king on one side and the queen on the other. Some scholars think this shows influence from Indian religions, where many-headed, many-armed gods are common. But although Kush probably conducted some trade with India, this drawing is more likely a gifted artist's way of showing someone doing many things at once.

In Praise of Lions

In a hymn of praise written in Egyptian on one temple wall, Apedemek is called "Lion of the South, strong of arm, great god . . . who will not be hindered in heaven and earth, who provides nourishment for all men, who hurls his hot breath against the enemy, the one who punishes all who commit crimes against him, who prepares a place for those who give themselves to him, who gives to those who call to him, Lord of life."

Statues of lions were placed around temples and guarded some of the reservoirs that were so important to the nomadic herdsmen. But real lions were also part of the religion. They were apparently kept in the temples and paraded before the public in religious processions. Pictures on temple walls show lions sniffing lotus flowers or being serenaded by musicians, and one wonders if this gives a glimpse of the luxurious life of a temple lion.

Apedemek must have been particularly popular in southern Kush. After all, he was local, and a victorious warrior god would have been a favorite among people continuously threatened by hostile tribesmen. Lions were frequent figures on Meroitic jewelry, armor, and horse harnesses, and a lion's head replaced the usual Egyptian cobra on some Meroitic crowns.

Other southern gods appeared in Meroitic times. The elephant, though perhaps not a god, was clearly important, and a large temple at Musawwarat seems to have been used for an elephant cult. Several other gods and goddesses not known from Egypt appeared in Kush or Kushite Nubia. These include a god named Sebewyemeker; Arensnuphis, another god associated with the lion; and an African-appearing goddess whose name has been lost.

The Divine King

In Egypt, the king was more than ruler of the state; he was also a god. When the heir to the throne became king, it was believed, he also became one with the hawk god Horus. When he died, he became one with Horus's father, Osiris, lord of the afterworld. His heir, in turn, became one with Horus, ruling the world of the living. This belief did a lot to strengthen the authority of the king and made it easier to run a complex government and military.

Kush took on many of the trappings of Egyptian kingship, particularly during the Twenty-fifth Dynasty, when the rulers wanted to prove themselves to their Egyptian subjects. It is not certain, however, that the Kushites adopted the belief in a divine king.

But even if not officially divine, the ruler of Kush was certainly considered the choice of the gods and was often called the child of Isis or Amon. The king or queen was also an important contact between the people of Kush and their gods. Along with the priests, rulers could speak for the gods. They could also speak for the people to the gods asking for protection against enemies or for good harvests and abundant rain.

This difference in Egyptian and Kushite attitudes about the king might reflect the more African way the rulers of Kush reached the throne. The oldest son of the king did not automatically become the next king, as usually happened in Egypt. Kushite inheritance passed through the female line, so the king's successor might be another child of the king's mother, or a child of his sister (who might also be his wife). Selection from among these many choices was often made by the priests or the army.

Horus, seen here in his temple at Edfu in Egypt, was a god of both Kush and Egypt. He was the divine representation of kingship and here wears the unified crown of upper and lower Egypt, a crown that the kings of Kush also claimed.

Remarkably, this system seemed to have worked fairly smoothly. No doubt there were political fights and family squabbles, but during the thousand years when Kush was ruled from Napata and Meroe, the kingship seems to have been passed down through the same royal family. And it is possible that this family traced its roots back to Kerma and even earlier. Whether the people of Kush thought their rulers divine or not, they must have felt that they had divine favor. A single ruling family lasting that long is very rare in the history of the world.

The Afterlife

Since the people of the Nile did not look kindly on change, a perfect life to them was pleasant, predictable, and free of disruptions. It isn't surprising, then, that when they thought about life after death, they didn't want a glorious new existence, but a continuation of the old one.

To reach the afterlife, it was necessary to have lived justly in this world. The ancient Egyptians and Kushites believed that, after death, Anubis, the jackal-headed god, weighed the dead person's heart against the feather of *Ma'at*, rightness. If the heart was weighted down with evil deeds, it was gobbled up by a creature who was part lion, part hippopotamus, and part crocodile. The person's soul would then die forever.

Souls that reached the afterlife could look forward to an eternal existence much like the one they had left. To help make this possible, food and drink were buried with the dead person along with some of his or her favorite jewelry, furniture, weapons, and cosmetics. As extra insurance, pictures of these things were painted inside the tombs of royalty and wealthy people

In this Egyptian tomb painting (ca. 1160 B.C.E.), the soul of Prince Hunefer is weighed against the feather of Ma'at, or truth. Anubis, guide of the dead, sets the scale while Thoth, god of scribes, records the result, and "the devourer" waits to gobble up the soul if it proves too heavy. Kushites shared this belief in divine judgment after death.

to be magically made real in the afterworld. And for people used to having servants, real servants or model ones were placed in their tombs as well.

The Egyptians also thought it was necessary to mummify the dead so that the soul could visit a well-preserved body and enjoy the provisions left in the tomb. Kushite royalty began using mummification while they ruled Egypt and continued with it during the Napatan and Meroitic years. Most of the common people of Kush, however, did not bother with making mummies.

Religious beliefs are always difficult to reconstruct just from the archaeological record. This is especially true when people did not write or when their writing cannot be read.

What is sometimes more revealing than ruins or writing is the fact that we are all human, whether we live now or in Kush. Many of the things ancient people enjoyed, thought, or feared are the same things that concern us. That makes it easier for us to look at the things people left behind and understand what they felt and how they lived.

CHAPTER FOUR

TRIUMPHS, TEMPLES, AND TOMBS

Today, many people are fascinated by pyramids and mummies. When we read about the ancient peoples of the Nile, it sometimes seems that they spent most of their lives thinking about gods and death. They might seem like very gloomy people.

But this is not a fair picture. When we study an ancient people, we usually learn more about their tombs and temples than about their marketplaces, schools, or even their homes. This isn't because tombs and temples were so much more important to people then, but because generally things meant to survive for eternity were built of longer-lasting materials.

In this nineteenth century lithograph, sand engulfs the great temple at Abu Simbel. It was built by Ramses II around 1250 B.C.E., when Egypt controlled Nubia.

A nineteenth-century artist recorded this view of the great temple at Philae, sacred to both Kush and Egypt.

The peoples of the Nile probably didn't spend any more of their time brooding about death than do most people. True, they went to a lot of trouble to ensure that they had a life after death, but that was because they loved life so much. The temples were there because it was important to keep the gods happy and maintain an order and balance. But most ordinary people probably paid little attention to them except on special days.

Restoring *Ma'at*

The rulers, of course, had to pay a lot of attention to the gods, because kings and queens were responsible for the welfare of their people. One of a ruler's most important duties was to maintain *Ma'at*, the divine order of things.

The kings of Kush who invaded Egypt and formed the Twenty-fifth Dynasty weren't just playing power politics. Sharing so much history and religion with their northern neighbor, they felt very close to Egypt. With Egypt's government falling apart and being run largely by foreigners, something seemed very wrong in the Nile Valley. Clearly, proper balance and order had to be restored, and Kush saw itself as just the young, vigorous kingdom to do that.

A stone statue of Senkamanisken shows the Napatan king wearing the two cobras of Kushite royalty, marking the royal claim to continue rule over both Kush and Egypt.

When they marched into Egypt, the kings of Kush didn't think of themselves as foreign conquerors. They were there to throw out the foreigners and restore the old ways. They worshiped the Egyptian gods with all the proper ceremonies. They added to temples and built new ones, even using older styles to show how they admired Egypt's traditions. They also put up lots of inscriptions so everyone would know they were behaving as Egyptian kings should.

The people of Egypt generally agreed that these Kushite kings were doing a good job. After many years of weakness and foreign domination, they welcomed the Twenty-fifth Dynasty as restorers of true Egyptian ways. Once the Kushites were overthrown, and Egypt eventually fell back under weak rulers and foreign control, the Egyptian people looked back at the Twenty-fifth Dynasty as golden years. They referred to the Kushite kings as having been just and wise, and they used the same terms for the descendants of those kings who continued to rule in distant Napata and Meroe.

A Land Set with Temples

In the end, the rulers of Kush failed to retain *Ma'at* in all of the Nile Valley, but once back in Kush, they were determined to keep things properly ordered in their own land. In part, this meant building temples to the gods.

Temples were the places where the gods could be worshiped, praised, and given offerings so they would meet the needs of their mortal subjects. Often a god was thought of as actually living in a special statue in his temple. In Egypt—and apparently in Kush, as well—the priests clothed, washed, and fed the statue and took it out to parade in front of the public on holidays. The most important gods had large temples and many priests, so additional people were needed to provide food for the temples and meet their other needs.

Most schooling also took place in temples, though royal children probably had special tutors. Reading and writing were used mostly in religion or government rather than in daily life, and it was generally priests who taught these skills. Wealthy families may have sent at least one child to the temples for schooling or to be trained to become a priest or priestess.

At first, the style of temples built in Kush resembled a main Egyptian type. These were generally long, rectangular buildings with pillared halls in the front and the altar and more sacred rooms in the back. Sometimes small

IF YOU LIVED IN ANCIENT KUSH

If you had been born in Kush around the time of King Netokamani and Queen Amanitare (12 B.C.E.–12 C.E.), your way of life would have been determined by the facts of your birth—whether you were a girl or a boy, wealthy or poor. With this chart, you can trace the course your life might have taken if you were a member of an ordinary family.

You were born in Meroe. . . .

As a Boy . . .

As a Girl . . .

You live in one of many mud-brick houses on a mound outside the royal walls. On hot nights, you and your family sleep on the flat roof to catch the Nile breezes. You don't wear much except a string of good luck charms, and you spend time playing with your friends, your dog, and your toys of clay and wood. On festival days, you love watching the parade of royalty and priests.

By the time you are six, one brother is at the temple learning to read and write; another brother wants to be a soldier; and you are an apprentice to your father, a potter. You work in his shop east of town turning the potter's wheel for him. Sometimes you use extra clay to make toys.

▼

As a teenager, you are making pots yourself and enjoy thinking up designs to paint on them. Sometimes you go into the hills near the royal pyramids to collect the white clay that makes the best pots. You'd like to marry the daughter of the blacksmith whose shop is near your father's, and already your families are making arrangements.

▼

As a man, you run the potter's shop, and your pottery is used in the palace and several temples. You like to take your children hunting using a throwing stick or bow and arrows. This year you are taking your family on the pilgrimage to Musawwarat to see the sacred elephants.

By the time you are six, you dress in a white cotton robe with colored designs. Your mother is teaching you how to make millet into bread, porridge, and beer. She is also showing you how to coil clay into cooking pots and decorate them with designs her mother taught her. You kept having trouble with your eyes, so the doctor put three cuts in your cheek. It hurt, but now you are proud of the scars—just like the king's!

▼

As a teenager, your facial scars make you pretty, and your mother thinks you should find a rich husband. But you like a young farmer you met at the market, and your mother admits he does treat her with respect as a future son-in-law should.

▼

As a woman, you have married the farmer and live south of town. You make cheese from the milk of cows and goats and trade it at the market for other goods. One of your daughters wants to marry a handsome herdsman she met at the Musawwarat festival, but you would rather she marry the carpenter's son, and usually you have the final word in family matters.

When you die, your family buries you on a bed along with food, drink, and some of your favorite things. They hold a feast where people cry and mourn but also dance and sing, because they miss you but know that you are going to a good life and they will meet you again.

The kiosk in front of the Lion Temple at Naga shows a unique Kushite mixture of Egyptian and Roman architectural styles.

buildings, or kiosks, were built in front of the main temples for certain ceremonies. The great Amon temples at Jebel Barkal near Napata and at Meroe are good examples of this style.

As time went on, other styles became popular, too. The sun temple at Meroe is an example of a basically square type where the sacred sanctuary is in the center surrounded by halls, platforms, or courts with pillars.

Kushite artists and architects, though liking tradition, were also willing to experiment. Greek and possibly even Indian and Persian influences can be seen in some of their work. Roman and Egyptian styles combined in the Lion Temple kiosk at Naga, an important religious site in a *wadi* east of Meroe.

The most unusual temple complex in Kush was at Musawwarat, located in another large *wadi* to Meroe's east. Construction began there in the sixth century B.C.E., and buildings were added over the years until it became a huge complex of temples, corridors, and courtyards. No large settlement has been

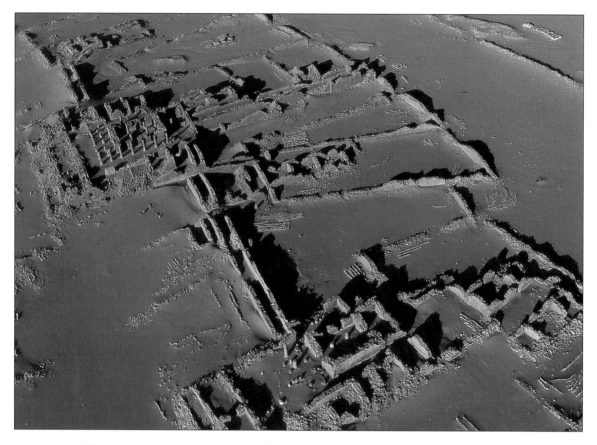

This aerial photograph of the temple ruins at Musawwarat shows the large enclosures where elephants may have taken part in ceremonies or prepared for war.

found in the area, so perhaps it was mostly a religious center to which worshipers traveled for special celebrations. The large reservoir there suggests that the site was also a center for nomadic herdsmen and a stopping place for caravans traveling to and from the Red Sea.

The special feature of Musawwarat is its relationship to elephants. Elephants are carved on walls, stone elephants and lions hold up pillars, and a life-sized elephant statue ends a wall in one of the courtyards. Because of the unusual way the temple is built with terraces, ramps, and large enclosures, live elephants may have been kept there as well.

It is not certain that the people of Kush actually believed in an elephant god, but elephants clearly had some sacred role. And elephants were important to Kush in other ways. Ivory was exported, but so were live elephants.

Elephants were not only used by Kush's army; they were provided to others as well. Egypt's Ptolemies used Kushite war elephants and trainers in their battles in Syria and elsewhere. At the time, wild elephants still lived around Musawwarat, and it could have been there that the war elephants of Kush were trained.

In prehistoric times, elephants lived throughout the Nile Valley but, by the time Egyptians started writing their history some five thousand years ago, elephants were considered creatures of the south. Egyptians never developed an elephant cult such as we see at Musawwarat.

Without written records, we cannot be sure what happened at Musawwarat, but we can imagine. For festival days, people wearing their

Elephants played an important role in the religious ceremonies at the temple at Musawwarat. Elephant figures are found on wall reliefs and architectural features, such as column bases. Here, a life-sized statue forms the end of a wall.

best clothes must have traveled there from the river towns of Kush. They walked or rode horses, donkeys, or an occasional camel. Nomadic herdsmen flocked there, too, and soon tents and huts surrounded the temple complex. In a procession of chariots, the royal family would arrive, their colorful robes and gold jewelry flashing in the sun, while servants fanned away the desert heat with ostrich-feather fans.

Then the priests would lead forth the sacred elephants. The day would pass with religious ceremonies, chanting, and dancing. Incense would fill the air along with the music of drum, harp, and flute, and partying would go on late into the night. We can be certain about the partying, at least, because a large number of cooked cattle bones and broken beer and wine jugs have been found.

Preparing for Eternal Rest

Even in prehistoric times, the people of the Nile clearly believed in life after death and the idea that things from this life would be useful afterward. The dead were carefully laid to rest along with some of their personal possessions and containers of food and drink.

In Egypt, people became particularly concerned that everything needed in the afterlife be provided in the grave. If the dead person was to be spared having to work in the afterlife, servants would have to be sent along, too. At first, the Egyptians did what was done elsewhere along the Nile; they killed real servants and buried them with important dead people. But early on, the servants were replaced by paintings of servants or by *shwabtis* (SHWAB-tees), little models of servants meant to come magically to life in the afterworld and do the required work.

The Egyptians also thought it important that the actual body be preserved in the tomb so that the soul could visit it and enjoy the spirit value of all the provisions left there. This led to the practice of mummification, at least for the wealthy. After the internal organs of the dead person were removed and placed in special jars, the body was dried in salt, drenched in preserving fluids, wrapped in cloths along with magical charms, and put in one or more mummy cases painted with the likeness of the dead person.

South of Egypt, however, the basic ideas were taken in different directions. The C Group Nubians put goods in the grave, but they didn't seem concerned that the body be preserved. Instead of mummifying the body and

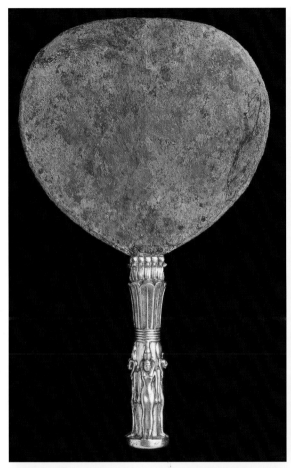

From the tombs of the Kushites: When this bronze mirror with a silver handle was polished, it reflected the face of its owner, Shabako, King of Kush and Egypt from 716 to 701 B.C.E. Men of Kerma were proud of their warrior skills and were often buried with weapons, either full size or miniature ones like this bronze dagger with a gilt handle, made around 1700 B.C.E. This jug from Napata around 600 B.C.E. shows the skill and good humor of Kushite potters.

placing it in a casket, they dressed the dead person in his finest jewelry and leather clothes, and laid him in the grave on his side as if asleep.

In Kerma, the body was laid on its side on a bed. This was also done in the early graves near Napata, and figures of Bes, the ugly little guardian of the bedroom, were often left in the tomb along with the other charms and offerings.

When the kings of Kush became kings of Egypt during the Twenty-fifth Dynasty, they took up mummification. This continued for royalty and other important members of the court even when the capital moved to Meroe. But some of these mummies were placed on beds, and plain bed burials or ones where the dead person was simply laid in the grave on his side continued to be used by ordinary Kushites.

This African tradition seems to have been very deeply rooted. Bed burials continued in Sudan after the fall of Meroe. Even today, after centuries

A few of the more than one thousand stone shwabtis *ready to do the work assigned to Twenty-fifth Dynasty King Taharqa once he reached the afterworld.*

of Christianity and then of Islam, Nubians are often carried to their graves on beds, and bowls for offerings are placed outside.

The idea of having models or paintings substitute for real grave offerings seems to have been more Egyptian than Kushite. The C Group people did put clay models of cattle, sheep, and goats in the graves, but a large number of cattle bones have also been found outside. At Kerma, hundreds of cattle were buried around the graves of dead rulers. And the people of Kerma did not use *shwabtis*, model servants, to do work in the afterlife. They used the real thing. Several hundred people were buried in the tombs with some of Kerma's rulers.

When the Twenty-fifth Dynasty Kushite kings took on Egyptian ways, they substituted *shwabtis* for servants. King Taharqa's tomb had more than a thousand stone *shwabtis*, some carrying little tools, ready to do any work required of the king. However, the Napatan kings were still buried with their favorite horses. When the royal family moved its burials to Meroe, they went back to older traditions. *Shwabtis* disappeared from the graves, and real people again accompanied their royal masters along with horses, cattle, dogs, and even camels.

Diodorus, the Greek historian, wrote about this tradition in the first century B.C.E., saying it was "customary for the comrades of the king even to die with him of their own accord and that such a death is an honorable one and proof of true friendship." He added that "it is for that reason that a conspiracy against the king is not easily raised . . . all his friends being concerned both for his safety and their own."

Housing the Dead

Throughout history, most of the ordinary people along the Nile were buried under earth mounds. In Egypt of the Old Kingdom, kings started building rectangular structures of brick or stone over their graves. Soon these became stone pyramids with the burial chambers constructed inside and chapels for prayers and offerings to the dead built on the east. By New Kingdom times, however, royalty had stopped using pyramids, though some wealthy commoners put steep little pyramids over the doors of their tombs.

In Nubia, C Group people were buried under circular mounds, sometimes with low rock walls around them and offering chapels on their east. At Kerma, the mounds were larger and more elaborate, but they were still

ROYAL HORSE LOVERS

Horses were first introduced to Egypt by the Hyksos from western Asia around 1800 B.C.E. Afterward, during the New Kingdom, horse-drawn chariots were used by Egyptian royalty, nobility, and the armies. But it was the rulers of Kush and the Twenty-fifth Dynasty who proved to be the biggest horse lovers.

Chief among these was King Piankhy, who ruled from 751–716 B.C.E. In the inscription about his conquest of Egypt, Piankhy mentions horses at least a dozen times, frequently demanding tribute of the "finest horses" from the rulers he conquered. When he captured one city, he didn't bother to look at the local king's wives, whom he had won, but instead went to inspect the royal stable. He then scolded the defeated king for the poor condition of his horses.

Piankhy and the other kings of the Twenty-fifth Dynasty weren't just fond of horses in life; they took their favorites with them when they died. Beside the kings' graves near Napata, twenty-four horses were buried in teams of four. They were entombed standing, adorned with beads, silver collars, and plumes. Later, the rulers buried at Meroe also took their horses along, some of them wearing elaborate leather harnesses decorated with metal plaques and bells.

With the large territory Kush had to control, horses would have been very useful. But to the rulers of Kush, horses were more than just a means of transportation. They were prized possessions to be kept forever.

round as were the early graves near Napata. Then for a while, the walled burial mounds of royalty took on a rectangular shape, and by the time the kings of Kush were in control of Egypt, the mounds had become square and had grown into pyramids. This must have been another way for the kings of the Twenty-fifth Dynasty to show how "Egyptian" they were.

These pyramids of Kush, however, were different from the earlier Egyptian model. They were smaller and steeper, and the burial chamber was beneath the pyramid rather than within it. Offering chapels were still built on the east for funeral ceremonies and making offerings to benefit the dead person's spirit. Much of the artwork in these chapels was a mixture of Kushite and Egyptian ideas. Stone offering tables showed the usual Egyptian gods of the dead but were inscribed in the Meroitic language.

These royal Kushite pyramids near Napata were smaller and steeper than the Old Kingdom pyramids of Egypt. The dead were buried in rock-cut chambers under the pyramids rather than inside the pyramids themselves.

The sandstone blocks used for the pyramids were quarried out of the hills just east of the royal cemeteries. The quality of workmanship and the use of stone or brick varied with the importance of the person buried and the prosperity of the times. Yet even now, after centuries of decay, a line of pyramids crowning ridgetops near the ancient capitals of Kush makes clear the link the rulers felt with Egypt.

While the royal family chose to be buried under pyramids, the ordinary people, even the townspeople of Meroe itself, followed more deeply African traditions. Laid to rest on beds and accompanied by grave goods and occasional sacrifices, their low round graves dotted the lands along the Nile.

Popular Beliefs

History always tells us more about rulers than about the people they ruled. It is usually the political or religious leaders who left the written records, built the monuments, or could afford goods that last through time. Archaeology

Wall paintings must once have decorated Kushite palaces and temples, but few have survived today. This one, showing a young man carrying baby elephants or elephant figures, may be based on a now-forgotten folktale.

helps, but it is hard to know exactly how ordinary people lived in antiquity or what they thought.

Still it seems that the people of Kush and their rulers shared the same worldview, believed in the same gods, and participated in the same public festivals. They were, after all, dependent on the same natural forces: the Nile and the sun. And they were subject to the same threats: hostile neighbors, sickness, and death.

Some gods may have been especially popular with ordinary citizens, gods who watched out for their daily needs or occupations or who were protectors like Apedemek, the "local god made good." Various charms were worn to ensure good luck and health. Children, particularly, wore figures of the god Bes, the squat, impudent protector of bedroom and children. And, probably, stories about the gods and their wonderful or funny doings were favorite after-dinner tales. Unfortunately, little of Kushite mythology has come down to us today.

The people of Kush knew rough times, as any people do, but basically theirs was a good life. Since they believed that their gods made this possible, they did all the traditional things to keep divine favor—performing the proper ceremonies, making offerings, and wearing charms. In this way, they were doing their part in maintaining *Ma'at*, in keeping centuries of divine order along the valley of the Nile.

CHAPTER FIVE

THE LEGENDS AND LEGACY OF KUSH

Kush is not as well known now as some ancient civilizations, but it deserves to be. In its time Kush was a great civilization and a vital part of its own world. Its culture thrived for several thousand years, and though the temples and kings are gone, much of the life lived by the people of Kush is still shared by people living along the Nile and in the rest of Africa.

In the ceremonies, the house types, the games, the pottery, and in many objects and attitudes, we see Kush alive throughout Africa. Even many of those things in Kush that seem most Egyptian, were themselves African in origin.

Archaeologists have been digging up the remains of ancient Kush for many years. This excavation, of the royal palace at Jebel Barkal, took place in 1996.

Archaeologists uncover a ram statue in front of the great Amon Temple at Jebel Barkal in 1989.

Why doesn't Kush receive the historical recognition it deserves? For one thing, until the Meroitic language can be read, the written record the later Kushites left of themselves will remain silent. Secondly, Kush developed on the fringes of the "civilized world." Travelers who might have written about it were often kept from Kush by distance, deserts, and impassable cataracts.

Finally, there is the fact that much of the world's history has been recorded by non-African people. Their attention is usually focused on their

HUTS IN HISTORY: THE AUTHOR'S OBSERVATIONS

In 1969, I helped at the University of Khartoum's excavations at Meroe. For several seasons, the workers had been digging through the tallest part of the city mound. We'd cut through more than thirty feet of dirt, household rubbish, and mud-brick walls, carefully recording everything we found. Finally we reached the bottom and were toweling the surface above when we noticed odd splotches down below in the soil.

From the edge of the excavation, we could make out a pattern of dark spots forming a circle and straight lines. This, we realized, was the remains of an ancient hut. The spots were where the wooden poles had been stuck into the earth. It was a round hut like those shown on the Karanog bowl or on the wall of the nearby sun temple.

When the Sudanese workers understood what it was, they said things like, "Oh, yes, that is where they did their cooking. The man slept on that side and the woman on the other, and that was a fence where they tied up the baby goats."

Sure, the rest of us thought. There's no way these guys could know such things about a hut built three thousand years ago.

Then came Christmas. It was a holiday, so we English and American archaeologists rode camels out to visit the sheik of the tribe to which many of our workers belonged. When we reached his round tent and he welcomed us in, we realized how his people could know so much about life three thousand years in the past. Many things had not changed. There, in the same spot as in the ancient hut, was where they cooked. The sheik slept on the same side to which the excavation workers had pointed, and his wife slept on the other. And there, in the same spot to the right of the door, was a fence with bleating baby goats tied to it.

Sometimes even archaeologists need to wake up and see the history living around them.

The author in 1969 near the quarries where the stone was taken for Meroe's pyramids, seen in the background.

own historical traditions, and they fail to give Africa and its achievements due recognition.

But in recent years, this has been changing. Archaeologists, linguists, and historians are pushing back the sands, the silence, and the neglect of centuries. They are giving us all a clearer picture of a once-great civilization. The people of modern Sudan are developing a strong pride in their heritage and are helping in this effort.

A Land of Legend

Even in its own time, Kush was an object of mystery and fascination for many. Exotic trade goods came from there. Kush was the land of gold, emeralds, and ivory. Leopard skins, ostrich eggs, and incense came from Kush, and so did those magnificent elephants. But not many people traveled to or from distant Napata or Meroe. The things that were known or imagined about Kush grew in people's minds until they became legends.

After the end of the Twenty-fifth Dynasty, when Egypt suffered periods of weakness and foreign control, the Egyptian people looked back fondly on the Kushite kings, and their reputation for wisdom and justice grew. This attitude spread around the Mediterranean, even to people who had no direct contact with Kush. Foreigners often referred to Kush by the general term *Ethiopia*, a name used today for an African country east of Sudan. Classical writers called these *Ethiopians* wise, just, blameless, and long lived.

In the ancient world, *wisdom* often included control over the magic arts. A popular story recorded in Ptolemaic Egypt tells of a Kushite magician so powerful that he was able to whisk away an Egyptian king in his sleep, fly him through the air to Meroe, flog him five hundred times in front of the king of Kush, and return him, black and blue, to his bed before sunrise.

The story goes on to describe how fifteen hundred years later, this same long-lived Kushite magician, along with his powerful magician mother, returns dramatically to Egypt for a magic duel with Egypt's chief magician.

Other popular legends in Ptolemaic Egypt and much of the ancient world revolved around Alexander the Great. This conquering Greek king did some remarkable things in life, but after his death, even more fantastic stories grew up about him. In one, he disguises himself so he can sneak into Kush and demand of "Queen Candace" the return of treasures she had taken from Egypt.

To reach Kush, Alexander has to pass through crystal mountains where there are fruit trees guarded by huge serpents. At Meroe, he sees a marvelously built royal palace, its furniture made of gold and jewels. The queen herself "was more beautiful in appearance and had more understanding than other women in the world." Her beauty is so great that it makes the great soldier cry. Among the marvels Candace shows Alexander is a special room of glowing stone and rare woods that is mounted on wheels and pulled by elephants whenever she wants to travel. The two rulers get along quite well, and eventually Alexander returns to his people with the booty and a great respect for Kush and its queen.

Elephants also figure in a novel written by the Greek Heliodorus, probably in the second century C.E., though it takes place centuries earlier. These were war elephants used by the king of Kush in a border fight with the Persian king then ruling Egypt. The Persians are definitely the bad guys here, and the Kushites not only have elephants, but they also have master archers and a king who is just, wise, and kind.

The heroine of this complicated adventure is a Meroitic princess who is also exquisitely beautiful and herself a skilled archer. She has been missing for years from Meroe, but her identity is at last revealed when an inscription in the strange Meroitic script is read. This author, too, stresses the fabulous wealth of Kush where emeralds are abundant and prisoners are bound in chains of gold.

Clearly Kush made an impression in the ancient world, even when truth was blended with a good deal of fantasy. Over the centuries, some of these legends survived. The nineteenth-century opera, *Aida*, is a tale of another beautiful Kushite princess, and in his once popular adventure novels, Victorian author Rider Haggard writes of a gorgeous and immortal queen ruling over a secret African realm whose rituals seem very Egyptian.

Legacy of Iron

At one time, scholars thought that those things in Africa's culture that were similar to ancient Egypt's must have come from Egypt and been introduced to the rest of Africa through Kush. Today, many believe that these similarities

AIDA, PRINCESS OF KUSH

Myths of Egypt and Kush survived even into European grand opera of the nineteenth century. To celebrate the opening of the Suez Canal in 1869, the ruler of Egypt commissioned Giuseppe Verdi, the great Italian composer, to write an opera.

Verdi chose as his setting ancient Egypt at a time of war with Kush. Aida, the heroine (as in Heliodorus's novel), is a lovely Kushite princess held captive in Egypt. She and her father, the disguised but powerful king of Kush, sing arias and duets about the beauty and wonders of their native land. Aida loves an Egyptian general who is convicted of treason for trying to help Aida and her father escape. In the end, the two lovers die tragically together, buried alive under the temple of Isis.

Verdi played rather loose both with history and the details of Egyptian religion. But his interest wasn't in accuracy. It was in using spectacle and an exotic setting to enhance a truly grand opera. He succeeded. The costumes for this show are often breathtaking, and the sets can offer mighty throne rooms, towering temples, and even pyramids. Sometimes, with a nod to real history, live Kushite war elephants are brought on stage.

Seeing *Aida* may not teach a lot of history, but it gives a taste of the grandeur and the myths that rose from the ancient Nile.

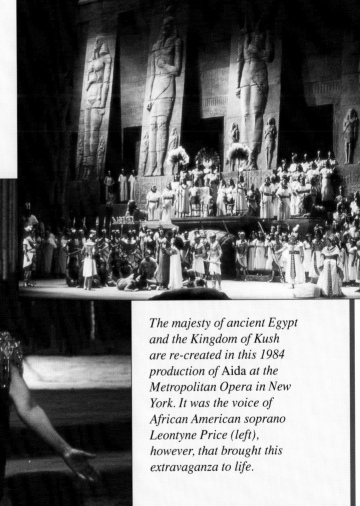

The majesty of ancient Egypt and the Kingdom of Kush are re-created in this 1984 production of Aida *at the Metropolitan Opera in New York. It was the voice of African American soprano Leontyne Price (left), however, that brought this extravaganza to life.*

Iron slag heaps east of the ancient city of Meroe. When a railway was cut through these mounds in the nineteenth century, scholars began to realize that Meroe must have been the location of an important early iron industry.

are there because ancient Egypt itself was an African culture and shared traits with Africa from the beginning. But in one matter, some scholars think that Kush may have influenced the rest of Africa: The continent's Iron Age is believed to have begun in Kush.

Iron ore is not found in Egypt. For over two thousand years, the metal that the Egyptians used for tools and weapons was copper and its alloy, bronze. Copper ore was abundant in Egypt. It could be worked fairly easily and hammered into shape while cold. The few iron objects Egyptologists have found from those early centuries were probably imports. In the tomb of Egypt's young King Tutankhamen, the iron toys, jewelry, and small iron dagger may have been treasured gifts from some foreign king.

When the Kushite armies conquered Egypt around 750 B.C.E., it was with the same kind of copper spear points, arrowheads, and swords used by the Egyptians. But in western Asia, iron ore had been discovered along with a method for heating it and hammering it into shape while still hot. This was important because iron tools and weapons were stronger and could remain sharp longer than implements of copper or bronze.

The kingdom of Assyria was so successful in conquering its neighbors, including Kushite Egypt, partly because its armies had iron weapons. Though

Modern blacksmiths in Karima, Sudan, use some ancient techniques to make and repair iron tools.

the Assyrians tried to keep iron their secret, more people began learning how to turn this dark rock into strong weapons.

And here Kush discovered an unexpected advantage. Although the area around Napata, like Egypt, had no natural iron, iron ore was abundant around Meroe. Some of the Meroitic royal pyramids are even built on natural iron deposits. What is more, Meroe, unlike Napata, was within the belt of seasonal rainfall. This meant that enough trees grew in the area to provide fuel for smelting iron.

The iron industry had begun in Meroe by the mid-sixth century B.C.E. At first, iron objects were rare and valuable. Royalty wore iron jewelry, and one king was buried with an iron spearhead wrapped in gold. But eventually, ordinary tools were made from the metal, and the famous Kushite archers were equipped with iron-tipped arrows. Iron objects also became a Meroitic export.

Ironworking itself could be done in small, scattered sites, but at Meroe it was concentrated for generations in an area on the eastern edge of town. The furnaces were round, brick structures, and air was pumped into them using bellows made from covered bowls. These furnaces produced a lot of slag, the dark material left over from ironworking. Large slag mounds around Meroe, some of which are now cut through by the railroad, alerted early scholars to Meroe's importance as an ancient ironworking center.

A Turning Point in History

Meroe's production of iron was certainly important in the history of the Nile Valley, but the question still unanswered is: How important was it to the rest of the continent? This is of interest because the introduction of ironworking marked a turning point in the history of Africa. With the use of iron, African kingdoms grew in power and wealth. Iron Age cultures and their history became rich and complex.

All this may well have started from Meroe. Kush certainly had trade contacts with the rest of Africa, but no one knows if knowledge of ironworking also traveled along those routes. The dates for African ironworking, and the somewhat similar types of furnaces and bellows used, make this a possibility.

But whether or not Kush actually brought about Africa's prosperous Iron Age, it was certainly its earliest and most powerful participant. New

This elegant sculpture, a shwabti—*or magical servant—has come down to us from the tomb of King Taharqa, who died more than 2,500 years ago.*

technologies often change history, and there is no question that the introduction of iron-working changed the history of Africa. Kush, with its thriving Meroitic iron industry, was in the forefront of that change.

The Achievement of Greatness

Kush left a lasting legacy to the world. The events of its history, the artifacts it left, and the legends that it spawned are all of lasting importance. But perhaps its most important achievement is simply that it was there. In a continent whose achievements are often overlooked, Kush reached undeniable greatness.

Before Rome became a world-conquering empire, before the Chinese built their great wall, before the tribes of northern Europe learned to write, the African people of Kush raised a great civilization.

Its people controlled vast territory, built lasting monuments, developed their own writing system, made exquisite pottery, lived by complex beliefs, and mastered a technology that changed the face of a continent. Kush is a proud part of the heritage, not only of Africa, but of the entire world.

The Ancient African Kingdom of Kush: A Chronology

4000 B.C.E.	Farming begins in Nile Valley
3500–2000 B.C.E.	A Group culture in Nubia
3100 B.C.E.	Egypt becomes a united kingdom
2000–1550 B.C.E.	C Group and Kerma cultures in Nubia
1550–1085 B.C.E.	Egypt controls Nubia; Amon temple built near Napata
750 B.C.E.	Kashta begins conquest of Egypt and establishes Twenty-fifth Dynasty
671 B.C.E.	Assyria attacks Egypt
655 B.C.E.	Kushites driven out of Egypt
591 B.C.E.	Egypt attacks Napata; shortly afterward, political capital of Kush moved to Meroe
525 B.C.E.	Persian King Cambyses sends spies to Meroe
280 B.C.E.	Arakakamani moves religious capital of Kush from Napata to Meroe
24 B.C.E.	Amanirenas and Akinidad attack Roman Egypt; Napata attacked following year
20 B.C.E.	Treaty of Samos between Rome and Kush
12 B.C.E.–12 C.E.	Prosperous reign of Netakamani and Amanitar
61 C.E.	Roman Emperor Nero sends expedition to Kush
350 B.C.E.	Meroe falls to Ezana of Axum

GLOSSARY

A Group: Nubian farming and herding people who lived from 3500 to 2000 B.C.E.

alloy: a blend of several metals to produce properties the individual metals do not have

amulet: small object believed to give the wearer magical protection

C Group: Nubian people, largely cattle herders, who lived from 2000 to 1500 B.C.E.

cataracts: a stretch of river in which there are rocks or waterfalls

cult: a system of religious worship focusing on a particular deity

cursive: a writing system that is flowing, often connected

dynasty: a period during which a single family and its descendants rule

hieroglyphics: a writing system of picture-based symbols, more angular than cursive

inscription: a section of writing, often engraved into a surface

Kerma: a city and culture in Nubia between 2000 and 1500 B.C.E.; first recorded capital of Kush

Meroitic: having to do with the town of Meroe or the period when Meroe ruled Kush, 591 B.C.E.–350 C.E.

Napatan: having to do with the town of Napata or the period when Napata ruled Kush, 800–591 B.C.E.

nomads: people who keep on the move, usually making a living by hunting and gathering

Nubia: region along the Nile approximately between the first and fourth cataracts

Ptolemaic: having to do with the culture or period when Egypt was ruled by the descendants of Ptolemy, the Greek general

regalia: the emblems or decorations of royalty, such as special clothing and crowns

reliefs: raised pictures carved into hard surfaces

scribe: a person whose job is reading or writing records

slag: the glassy or porous residue left from smelting metal ore

wadi: an Arabic word for a stream valley that is usually dry except during rainy seasons

FOR FURTHER READING

Arkell, A. J. *A History of The Sudan to 1821.* London: The Athlone Press, 1961.

Bianchi, Robert Steven. *The Nubians: People of the Ancient Nile.* Brookfield, New York: The Millbrook Press, 1994.

Davidson, Basil. *The Lost Cities of Africa.* Boston: Little Brown and Co., 1959.

Haynes, Joyce L. *Nubia, Ancient Kingdoms of Africa.* Boston: Museum of Fine Arts, 1992.

Hintze, Fritz, and Ursula. *Civilizations of The Old Sudan.* Leipzig: Edition Leipzig, 1968.

Marston, Elsa. *The Ancient Egyptians.* New York: Marshall Cavendish, 1996.

Oliver, Roland, ed. *The Dawn of African History.* London: Oxford University Press, 1968.

Shinnie, Peter. *Meroe, A Civilization of The Sudan.* London: Thames and Hudson, 1967.

Shinnie, Margaret. *Ancient African Kingdoms.* New York: New American Library, 1965.

Taylor, John H. *Egypt and Nubia.* Cambridge, MA: Harvard University Press, 1991.

BIBLIOGRAPHY

Adams, William. *Meroitic North and South.* Berlin: Akademie Verlag, 1976.

Adams, William. "Pottery, Society, and History in Meroitic Nubia." In *Meroitica I.* Berlin: Akademie Verlag, 1973.

Ali Hakim, Akmed M. *Meroitic Architecture: A Background of an African Civilization.* Khartoum: University of Khartoum Press, 1988.

Bradley, Rebecca. "Varia from the City of Meroe." In *Meroitica VI.* Berlin: Akademie Verlag, 1982.

Erman, Adolf. *Handbook of Egyptian Religion,* Boston: Longwood Press, 1977.

Gardiner, Sir Alan. *Egypt of the Pharaohs.* Oxford: Clarendon Press, 1961.

Heliodorus. *An Ethiopian Romance.* Translated from the Greek by Moses Hadas, Ann Arbor: University of Michigan Press, 1957.

Ibrahim, al Nur Mohammed. *Life and Death in Meroe.* Khartoum: University of Khartoum Press, 1977.

Kendall, Timothy. "Ethnoarchaeology." In *Studia Meroitica.* Berlin: Akademie Verlag, 1989.

Kendall, Timothy. Kush, *Lost Kingdom of the Nile: A Loan Exhibition from the Museum of Fine Arts, Boston.* Brockton, MA: Brockton Art Museum, 1982.

Lichtheim, Miriam. *Ancient Egyptian Literature: A Book of Readings.* Vol. III. Berkeley: University of California Press, 1980.

Lucas, A. *Ancient Egyptian Materials and Industries.* London: Edward Arnold, 1962.

Mercer, Samuel. *Religion of Ancient Egypt.* London: Luzac and Company, 1949.

O'Connor, David. *Ancient Nubia: Egypt's Rival in Africa.* Philadelphia: University of Pennsylvania, 1993.

Pseudo-Callisthenes. *The Alexander Book in Ethiopia.* Translated by Sir Wallis Budge. London: Oxford University Press, 1933.

Robertson, John. "History and Archaeology at Meroe," *An African Commitment: Papers in Honor of Peter Lewis Shinnie.* University of Calgary Press, 1992.

Save-Soderborgh, T. "The Nubian Kingdom of the Second Intermediate Period." In *Kush* IV, 1956.

Shinnie, Peter, ed. *The African Iron Age,* Oxford: Clarendon Press, 1971.

Shinnie, Peter, and Rebecca Bradley. *The Capital of Kush: Meroe Excavations,* 1965–1972. Berlin: Akademie Verlag, 1980.

Shinnie, Peter, and Francois J. Kense. "Meroitic Iron Working." In *Meroitica VI.* Berlin: Akademie Verlag, 1982.

Trigger, Bruce. *History and Settlement in Lower Nubia.* New Haven: Yale University, 1965.

Zabkar, L.V. *Apedemek, Lion God of Meroe.* Warminster: Aris and Phillips, Ltd., 1975.

INDEX

Page numbers for illustrations are in boldface.